EARTHWA...

Booktalks and Activities

by Nancy Polette
illustrated by Paul Dillon

Copyright © 1993 by Nancy Polette

ISBN 1-879287-26-9

Book Lures Inc.

P. O. Box 0455
O'Fallon, MO 63366
1-800-844-0455

Printed in U. S. A.

EARTHWATCH: Booktalks and Activities for Grades 2-6

Contents

Earthwatch: Booktalks and Activities for Grades 2-6 by Nancy Polette

INTRODUCTION

"With so many problems facing our planet, you might not think that you can make a difference. But everything you do has an effect on the environment."
(From *Going Green* by John Elkington. Viking, 1990)

Earthwatch introduces a vitally important topic to students in grades two through six by using outstanding picture books in both fiction and non-fiction. The booktalks present enough of each book to get students thinking about and responding to the topic. If it is possible to have the books in the classroom, this is a real bonus! However, *Earthwatch* gives you enough information so that activities can be carried out using beginning encyclopedia research or other non-fiction books on the various topics.

The activities in *Earthwatch* were designed using what research say works! Compatible with a whole language philosophy, the activities draw from students' experiences, require risk taking and stress meaning and active involvement.

Earthwatch uses literature from outstanding authors and illustrators and literature activities stress predicting and confirming or denying predictions to foster student involvement in the learning process.

Students are encouraged to explore beyond the booktalks into a variety of non-fiction areas in social studies and science, working together cooperatively.

Skills arise naturally from the literature and are applied in the editing of final products.
A valuable addition to any science or social studies program, *Earthwatch* helps students to understand a vitally important topic and to explore and respond to the topic based on individual ability.

A Fact You Should Know

Most animal species become extinct because of things people do like cutting down forests and polluting rivers and lakes.
From: *Take Action* by Ann Love. Beech Tree, 1993.

Pre-Reading Activity: Before hearing the booktalk, match the animals below with their natural habitats. Guess if you do not know.

1. mountain   _____ chimpanzee
2. desert   _____ octopus
3. jungle   _____ hawk
4. ocean   _____ coyote

Booktalk

My Yellow Ball by Dee Lillegard. Illustrated by Sarah Chamberlain. Dutton, 1993.

Five times a little girl throws her yellow ball into the sky, each time throwing it farther than the last. At the first throw, the ball goes over the mountains where two hawks bat it back and forth over a cloudy net. The second throw takes the ball across a desert where a pack of coyotes scrambled after it. Next the ball soared into a jungle where chimpanzees chased and caught it. Then it sailed over the ocean where an octopus played catch with it. Finally the ball travels to outer space where it strikes a star for the little girl to wish upon. Wish she does, and soon she has a very good-and real-reason to throw her yellow ball again this time nice and easy.

Play The X Game!

Select a familiar animal name to write on the chalkboard. However, rather than letters, use Xs for the correct number of letters in the name.

EXAMPLE: X X X X tells those who are guessing that there are four letters in this animal's name. Students take turns guessing a letter. For example: a student might guess (correctly) that the third letter is W. This X is then erased and the letter W put in its place. If the student cannot then guess the animal, another student takes a turn in guessing another letter. A student can only guess the animal name if a letter is guessed correctly.

A Fact You Should Know

Unless we work to protect animals on the Earth, 25% of all that exist now will be gone within 20 years.

From: *Going Green* by John Elkington. Viking, 1990.

Pre-Reading Activity: Before hearing the booktalk about *Sister Yessa's Story*, see if you can place these animals in their correct setting. Put the number of the setting before each animal name. Guess if you do not know.

1. African Grasslands   2. Arctic Ocean   3. desert
4. Himalayas   5. Australia   6. Turtle Islands

_____ elephants   _____ snow leopards   _____ whales

_____ herons   _____ camels   _____ crabs

_____ cobras   _____ polar bears   _____ yaks

_____ dingoes   _____ koala bears   _____ lions

Booktalk

Sister Yessa's Story by Karen Greenfield. Illustrated by Claire Ewart. HarperCollins, 1992.

As storm clouds gathered Sister Yessa led the animals, two by two, to her brother's place. On the way she told the story of Great Turtle who, many years ago, walked the Earth with all of the world's animals on its back. As Great Turtle passed the African Grasslands, he stumbled and elephants and lions slip off his back. At the edge of the Arctic Ocean, Great Turtle slipped on the ice dumping whales and polar bears into the icy sea. In a hurry to reach water in the hot, dusty desert, turtle stumbled, leaving camels and cobras behind. Quenching his thirst high in the Himalayas, turtle left behind snow leopards and yaks. And in Australia, by the light of the stars, turtle found a home for the koala bears and dingoes. Then turtle paused. Where would he live? He chose the Turtle Islands, of course, and made his home with the crabs and the herons. Just as Sister Yessa finished her story and arrived at her brother's place, the rain began to fall. "Welcome," said her brother. "Come in out of the rain." Can you guess her brother's name? If you are not sure, read *Sister Yessa's Story*.

Sister Yessa's Story (continued)

A Writing Activity

I. Choose one of the animals mentioned in *Sister Yessa's Story* and find information about the animal to complete the data bank below.

Data Bank - Crabs

Eats
other small
shell creatures

Lives
ocean
deep water
tidal streams

Looks Like
big bug
walking scissors

Has
hard shell
jointed legs

Does
swims
paddles

II. Use your information to write a compare/contrast report about the animal.

EXAMPLE:

If I had the claws of a crab

I would paddle in the ocean

And catch other small shelled creatures

But I wouldn't squirt ink

Because an octopus does that.

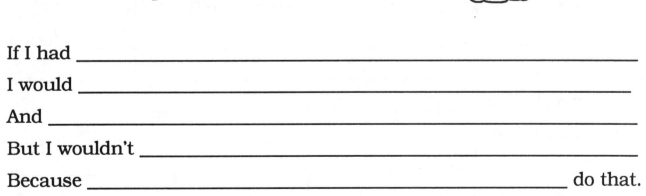

If I had _____

I would _____

And _____

But I wouldn't _____

Because _____ do that.

> ## A Fact You Should Know
> Animals now living on the Earth are disappearing 10,000 times faster than they did before humans arrived on the Earth.
> From: *Protecting Endangered Species* by Felicity Brooks. Usborne, 1990.

The Desert

Pre-Reading Activity: Work with a partner or small group to answer the following questions before hearing the booktalk. *Guess* if you do not know the answer. Question: What thing in the desert would do each of the following?

1. _____ bounce 2. _____ sing 3. _____ dart
4. _____ glide   5. _____ creep 6. _____ sting

Booktalk

Mojave by Diane Siebert. Paintings by Wendell Minor. HarperCollins, 1988.

> "I am the desert
>   I am free
>   Come walk the sweeping face of me."

Tumbleweeds bounce and roll along the ground. Lizards dart, tortoises creep, and snakes glide out of sight. The Mojave Desert is a special place. Its landscape is powerful and mesmerizing with deep arroyos, the windstorm's sting of sand and dust, the cry of the bold, black raven above ghost towns that lie with crumbling walls and the night songs of coyotes singing, "We are the desert, we are free." Here is an extraordinary celebration of this vast and ever changing wonder for nature lovers of all ages.

A Five Senses Poem

Write a five senses poem about the desert. Use the pattern that follows:

The desert is _____(color)

It looks like _____

It sounds like _____

It smells like _____

It tastes like _____

It makes me feel like _____

_____

A Fact You Should Know

When farmers turned the prairie lands of the West into fields for crops, the bison, the plains grizzly and the plains wolf became extinct.

From: *Take Action* by Ann Love. Beech Tree Books, 1993.

The Desert
Booktalk

Way Out West Lives a Coyote Named Frank by Jillian Lund. Dutton, 1993.

Meet Coyote Frank— he's one cool character, whether he's hanging out with his friends, chasing rabbits, mixing it up with a Gila monster, or pondering the setting sun. Frank chases skunks and digs up mouses' houses. He and his friend Larry think scorpions are scary and tortoises are tricky. Follow Frank and his friends through a typical day which ends with the thing coyotes like to do best, say hello to the moon.

A Writing Activity

Choose one of the desert animals mentioned in the book. Use the pattern below to write about the animal. Use factual information in your writing.

EXAMPLE: In the hot Arizona desert

By the Sabino Canyon stream

Between flat sandy rocks

Lives a rattlesnake named Rory.

Your Turn:

In the _____

By the _____

Between _____

Lives a _____ named _____

(Use other prepositions if you wish)

A Fact You Should Know
Many rivers have been polluted by factories dumping waste into them.

From: *Protecting Rivers and Seas* by Kamini Khanduri. Osborne, 1991.

The River Booktalk

Where the River Begins written and illustrated by Thomas Locker. Dial Books. 1984.

Josh, Aaron and grandfather set off on a camping trip to find the beginning of the river that flows past their farm, gentle, wide and deep. In the foothills the river narrowed and raced over rocks and boulders and then narrowed so much it seemed to disappear. Finally the river trickled into a small pond. In this small, peaceful place the river began. In the morning the river had swelled its banks from the storm the night before drawing its water from high in the mountains. As the boys' journey ends, the journey of the river continues as it always has, "flowing gently toward the sea."

Write a river song! Use names of creatures that make the river their home. Sing to the tune of "The Bear Went Over the Mountain."

EXAMPLE:
We saw a trout in the river
We saw an otter in the river
We saw a dragonfly by the river
For the river is their home.

We saw a _____ in the river

We saw a _____ on the river

We saw a _____ by the river

For the river is their home.

A Fact You Should Know

Each plant and animal on the Earth is suited to its living place. If the habitat changes, the animal and/or plant may not survive.

From: *Protecting Endangered Species* by Felicity Brooks. Usborne Pub. 1990.

Rivers

Pre-Reading Activity: Work with a small group or partner to respond to the following statement before hearing the booktalk. Suppose a river in Texas dried up. Name at least four sources of water the animals that depended on the river might find.

_____   _____

_____   _____

Booktalk

Alamo Across Texas by Jill Stover. Lothrop, Lee and Shepherd Books, 1993.

On the Lavaca River in the great state of Texas lived an alligator named Alamo. Life along the river suited Alamo perfectly, filled as it was with plenty of water, lots of tasty fishes, and a fine shade tree— until one year there came a drought. No more water. No more fishes. No more shade. So Alamo set off down the trail to find a new home. He walked and he walked and he walked and he walked until he came to a water trough on a Texas ranch but it was too small. He walked and he walked and he walked and he walked until he came to a too crowded swimming pool (with no tasty fishes) and a city fountain with too much noise. So Alamo left the city and walked to the end of the trail. Exhausted, he curled up under a cactus and went to sleep. But a great surprise awaits Alamo when he wakes up...to discover what it is, read *Alamo Across Texas*!

Rivers

Alamo Across Texas (continued)

Sing A Song About Alamo's Travels!

Sing to the tune of "Yellow Rose of Texas"

On the great (1) L_____ River

Alligator (2) A_____

Enjoyed the tasty (3) f_____

And watched the river (4) f_____ .

But a (5) d_____ dried up the river

Alamo with much remorse, went travelling throughout (6)

T_____

To find a water source.

He walked and (7) w_____ a distance,

At a ranch he saw some cattle.

The ocean was too (8) s_____

In the pool he had to (9) b_____.

The fountain was too (10) n_____

The water was not deep,

So at the end of a long, long (11) t_____

He curled up and went to (12) s_____.

Answer Key: 1. Lavaca 2. Alamo 3. fishes 4. flow 5. drought 6. Texas 7. walked 8. salty 9. battle 10. noisy 11. trail 12. sleep

8

Rivers
Alamo Across Texas (continued)

A Texas Spelling Lesson!

On small, separate pieces of paper, write these letters:

R A L A G I L O T

1. Alamo walked past an ___ ___ ___ well on his search for water. Use three of your letters to make the missing word.

2. Add one more letter to make a word that means work.
   ___ ___ ___ ___

3. Take away two letters and add two letters to name a kind of monster that is found in Texas. ___ ___ ___ ___

4. Take away one letter and add three letters to name something a Texas cowboy uses.
   ___ ___ ___ ___ ___

5. Use all of the letters to name an animal in the book, *Alamo Across Texas.*
   ___ ___ ___ ___ ___ ___ ___ ___ ___

6. How many other words can you make using the letters above?

   _____   _____

   _____   _____

   _____   _____

A Fact You Should Know

Early farmers drained wetlands to make room for fields. Wildlife disappeared and fields dried up. Today's farmers have stopped draining the prairie. Now there is water for crops and wildlife has returned.

From: *Take Action* by Ann Love. Beech Tree Books. 1993.

The Prairie

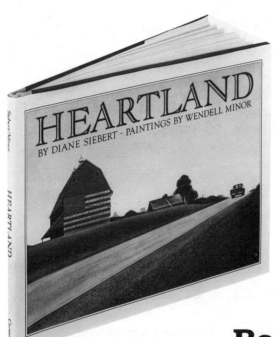

Guess! In the Heartland, name something that would:

a. wave
b. flow
c. stretch
d. graze
e. fill the barns

Listen to the booktalk to see which guesses were right!

Booktalk

Heartland by Diane Siebert. Paintings by Wendell Minor. HarperCollins, 1989.

"I am the heartland, great and wide. I sing of hope. I sing of pride." Welcome to America's Heartland— a place where golden wheat waves in the breeze, where great rivers flow, and cornfields stretch across the plains in glorious patchwork quilts of greens, yellows and browns. Cattle graze in lush green pastures, horses and sheep fill the barns, and a newborn calf stands damp and warm in the sun. This is the Heartland where the farmer is king, but over everything, Nature reigns supreme.

A Writing Activity

Look at the cover of this book. List (on separate pieces of paper) nouns, verbs, adjectives and adverbs related to the cover. After five minutes put your words together to create a sentence to describe the cover. You can add the noun determiners *a, an* and *the* and any needed prepositions to make your sentence.

A Fact You Should Know

About three thousand plants are eaten by people, but seven provide most of our food.

From: *Going Green* by John Elkington. Viking, 1990.

Mountains

Pre-Reading Activity: A Mountain Quiz

Answer each of the questions below. *Guess* if you are not sure of the answer. Then read or listen to the booktalk that follows to support or deny your guesses.

1. Sierra is the name of
   a. a mountain   b. a river   c. a tree
2. A California mountain chain has survived
   a. glaciers   b. earthquakes   c. neither   d. both
3. Mountain animals include
   a. bear   b. mountain lions   c. neither   d. both
4. A tree found in the Sierra Nevada chain is
   a. cherry   b. Sequoia   c. neither   d. both

Booktalk

Sierra by Diane Siebert. Illustrated by Wendell Minor. HarperCollins, 1991.

In *Sierra*, a giant rocky mountain speaks of beauty, life and endurance through the ages. It speaks in rhyme for itself, and for its tall sister peaks in the Sierra Nevada chain of mountains in California. They have survived glaciers and earthquakes. They support giant, centuries old sequoia trees. Predators such as bears and mountain lions hunt the wildlife they nurture. Now they stand as sentinels watching as the ultimate predator, man, threatens all they protect and nurture on their mountain sides.

Mountains
Sierra (continued)

A Writing Activity

Complete the following free verse (non-rhyming) poem. Choose any words you feel are appropriate.

I am a mountain rocky and _____

A tall spire, a sentinel seeing _____

_____

Within the shade of my rocky cliffs I shelter _____

_____

and _____

I am strong, stronger than _____

_____ that try to wear me down.

I am a mountain looking on as man approaches with _____

_____

Feeling fear as man _____

_____

Yet, harboring hope as others _____

_____

My name is Sierra.

Mountains Booktalk

The Mountain written and illustrated by Peter Parnall. Doubleday, 1971. (Grades K-4)

"These are the birds that lived in the trees that sheltered the deer that lived in the forest that grew on the mountain that stood in the west."

In these words the story is told of a single mountain in the West, a mountain on which flowers and trees grow and where birds, deer and many other animals live and find shelter. Along comes a group of people who love the mountain and want to keep it just the way it is. So, it is made a national park...and there the trouble starts. Trees are cut down, roads are built, campsites are established. And more and more people come to see the mountain and almost destroy it through littering and carelessness with campfires and matches.

A Writing/Research Activity

Choose a national park to write about.

Find out:
      1. Name
      2. Two physical features
      3. Three activities you can do there
      4. Four things you would see
      5. A descriptive phrase

Use this information to complete the pattern below.

Yellowstone

Geysers   Mountain Trails

Hike   Camp   Fish

Huge Trees   Old Faithful   Bears   Moose

Guardian of Wildlife

A Fact You Should Know

It takes 75,000 trees to make enough paper to run a Sunday edition of the New York Times.

From: *Going Green* by John Elkington. Viking, 1992.

The Forest

Question: How can you use a tree for woodcarving objects yet protect the tree at the same time?

This question arises in this readers theatre booktalk!

The Singing Fir Tree by Marti Stone. Illustrated by Barry Root. Whitebird Book, Putnam, 1992. (Grades 2-4)

Reading Parts:	Narrator One, Narrator Two, Pierre, Two to three villagers

Narrator One:	The singing comes to the village from high in the mountains
Villagers:	whenever the wind blows a certain way.
Narrator Two:	Then Pierre, the woodcarver, like everyone else in the village
Pierre:	stops work to listen to the lovely melody.
Narrator Two:	When Pierre discovers
Pierre:	that the singing comes from an ancient fir tree
Narrator Two:	he longs to cut it down and use it for his masterpiece, an ornate tower for the town's clock.
Villagers:	"But you can't cut the tree down,"
Narrator One:	shouted the villagers.
Villagers:	"Its singing has been a part of our village forever. You must find another tree."
Narrator Two:	But Pierre knew that
Pierre:	no other tree would do.
Both Narrators:	His masterpiece *must* come from this tree.

How can Pierre make this happen without cutting down the tree? Read *The Singing Fir Tree* to find out.

A Fact You Should Know
Preserving forests is essential for wildlife. Just one tree can be home to hundreds of birds, insects and mammals.
From: *The Environment* by Adam Markham. Rourke, 1988.

The Forest

Pre-Reading Activity: Before hearing the booktalk take this quiz about Indians and nature. *Guess* if you do not know the answer. Answer yes or no.

1. _____ Indians set the forests on fire to make good hunting grounds.

2. _____ Indians usually killed more than they needed for food and clothing.

3. _____ When the Indians set fires in the forest, the giant trees were the first to burn.

4. _____ Wars were fought over the destruction of the Indians' hunting grounds by the settlers.

Booktalk

The Land of Gray Wolf written and illustrated by Thomas Locker. Dial, 1991.

Many years ago a young Indian boy and his father, Gray Wolf, helped the rest of the tribe set fire to the forest. The fire burned the dry grass and dead wood, but moved too quickly to harm the giant trees. New spring grass then grew to provide a good hunting ground for the tribe. However, the Indians killed only wildlife that was needed for food and clothing.

White settlers moved into the area, cutting down the trees and destroying the hunting grounds. The Indians prepared for war. During one battle, Gray Wolf was killed and the village burned to the ground. Surviving members of the tribe were forced to go to a plot of land called a reservation. This book ends, however, with hope for the future in *The Land of Gray Wolf*.

The Forest
The Land of Gray Wolf (continued)
Writing About the Forest

You can use the pattern below to give factual information about the forest or you can use it as a creative writing activity. Before completing the pattern, list one word for each of the following:

1. A size _____
2. A color _____
3. An animal _____
4. A place to sleep _____
5. A human _____
6. A way to travel _____
7. Same human as #5 _____
8. Something to read _____
9. Same animal as #3 _____
10. Animal noise _____
11. Forest animal different from #3 _____
12. Different animal _____
13. Different animal _____
14. Human-same as #5 _____
15. Way to travel-same as #6 _____

Use the words you chose above in the numbered spaces in this story.

In the dark, grassy forest there was a 1) size _____ 2) color _____ 3) animal _____ who was sound asleep on a 4) place to sleep _____. A 5) human _____ approached on a 6) way to travel_____. The 7) human _____ was reading a 8) something to read_____ and stumbled over the 9) animal _____ who awakened and gave a loud 10) type of noise _____ that frightened the other forest animals including the 11) animal _____, 12) animal _____ and 13) animal _____. The 14) human_____ left quickly on the 15) way to travel_____ vowing never to disturb the forest animals again.

The Forest
The Land of Gray Wolf (continued)

Writing About Different Uses for Things in Nature

Nature provided the Indians with plants, animals and fish to make many useful things. From animals they made bearskin blankets or a deerskin pouch. From trees they made tools, canoes and torches. From stones they made arrowheads. Think of some useful things you could make using plants, rocks or trees.

I could use _____

to make _____, and

I would use it for _____.

I could use _____

to make _____, and

I would use it for _____.

I could use _____

to make _____, and

I would use it for _____.

A Mini Research Project

Look up trees in the encyclopedia. How many products can you find that are made from trees? Name as many as you can.

A Fact You Should Know

In the eastern United States farms and cities are gobbling up hardwood forests.

From: *Take Action* by Ann Love. Beech Tree, 1992.

The Forest

A Readers Theatre Booktalk

Song for the Ancient Forest by Nancy Luenn. Illustrated by Jill Kastner. Atheneum, 1993.

Reading Parts: Raven, Spirit, Little Girl, Narrator One, Narrator Two

Narrator One:	Long ago Raven
Raven:	dreamed that the forests were gone,
Narrator One:	and he asked for
Raven:	a song of power
Narrator One:	to change his dream.
Narrator Two:	The world's spirit answered,
Spirit:	"Every song must have a singer and each singer must find someone who understands his song."
Narrator One:	Raven sings the song
Raven:	about the death of the forest,
Narrator One:	but he is known as a trickster
Narrator Two:	and the people are reluctant to heed his warning. Finally a little girl
Little Girl:	understands the song
Narrator Two:	and manages to convince her father, a logger,
Little Girl:	to spread the word.
Narrator One:	Although Raven is killed
Raven:	in a confrontation between the loggers and the forest owner,
Narrator Two:	the trees themselves take up the song
Narrator One:	and Raven, the trickster, comes back to life.
All:	You won't want to miss this exciting tale *Song for the Ancient Forest.*

The Forest
Song for the Ancient Forest (continued)

Write a Forest Song

1. List plants and animals you would find in a forest.

   A. fir trees   B. rabbits   C. toads

   D. _____   E. _____   F. _____

2. Complete a pattern like this one. Sing the completed song to the tune of "Skip to My Lou".

   In the forest we see:

Green	fir trees	standing	in the shade
White	rabbits	nibbling	on the grass
Bumpy	toads	snatching	at a fly

   Look, little children, look.

   In the forest we see:

_____	_____	_____	_____
describe	name	ing word	where
_____	_____	_____	_____
_____	_____	_____	_____

   Look, little children, look.

> ## A Fact You Should Know
> Each year over 40 million acres of rain forest are destroyed through burning or logging and with this destruction we lose over 6000 species a year.
>   From: *The Rain Forest* by Helen Cowcher.

The Rain Forest

Pre-Reading Activity: Before hearing a booktalk about the Rain Forest, put an *A* before any word below that is an animal; an *O* before any word which is an object you would expect to see in a rain forest and an *N* before any word that names something you would not want to see in a rain forest. *Guess* if you are not sure.

1. _____ tapirs
2. _____ sloth
3. _____ flood
4. _____ trees
5. _____ macaw
6. _____ machine
7. _____ man
8. _____ canopy
9. _____ jaguar

Booktalk

The Rain Forest by Helen Cowcher. Farrar, Straus and Giroux, 1988.
    Many animals, plants and insects live in the rain forest. Among them are sloths, tapirs, jaguars, macaws and monkeys. They live in harmony until the day when man with his powerful machine comes to cut down the trees. The animals' fear causes them to seek high ground. Then the floods come forth with no trees to hold the soil in place the swirling water washes away man and his machine. Although the animals are safe on high ground as the story ends, we wonder, as they do, how long the tall trees will be there to protect them.

A Writing Activity

Write about one of the rain forest animals as an acrostic poem. See the example that follows:

M errily swinging from tree to tree
O ver the forest floor
N imble and active
K eeping watch day after day
E ager to warn
Y ou if danger comes.

> ## A Fact You Should Know
> Tropical rain forests are essential to maintain the Earth's climate.
>
> From: *Take Action* by Ann Love. Beech Time, 1992.

The Rain Forest

Pre-Reading Activity: A Rain Forest Quiz

Work with a partner to answer each question yes or no. *Guess* if you are not sure. Support or deny your guesses by listening to the booktalk that follows:

1. _____ A Kapok tree is a small, slender tree.

2. _____ The Amazon Rain Forest is in South America.

3. _____ Both the jaguar and the three-toed sloth can be found in the Amazon rain forest.

4. _____ The rain forest is very hot.

Booktalk

The Great Kapok Tree by Lynne Cherry. Harcourt, Brace, Jovanovich, 1990.

The tall, strong Kapok tree stood in the middle of the Amazon Rain Forest. One day a man came to this South American forest to chop the tree down. Before long, the heat and the hum of the forest lulled him to sleep. While he slept, each of the animals who lived in and around the tree murmured their pleas to him to not cut the tree down. The snake slithered down the tree. The jaguar appeared out of the dappled light of the forest floor, and a three-toed sloth climbed down from its forest canopy. The man awoke with a start and for the first time saw them for the wondrous creatures they were. He hesitated only a moment, then left the forest as untouched as he had found it.

The Rain Forest

The Great Kapok Tree (continued)

Pretend that you have a great tree in your backyard. Choose three living creatures that might live in or under the tree. Create a story about the tree and its inhabitants. Follow the pattern below.

THE GREAT _____ TREE

Come into my yard and see the great

_____ tree. In its branches you can see the

_____ who live there. _____

build nests on its sturdy limbs and _____

burrow under the bark.

   If the tree were not in my yard there would be no

_____ or

_____

and I would surely miss _____.

   So welcome to my great _____ tree!

A Fact You Should Know

If you could collect all the water that falls on one leaf in the rain forest for one year you would have a bathtub full.

From: *Take Action* by Ann Love. Beech Tree Books, 1992.

The Rain Forest

Pre-Reading Activity: Give A Good Guess!

Put a check mark beside any animal that you believe lives in the tropical rain forest. Listen to the booktalk to support or deny your guesses.

_____ sloth	_____ lizard	_____ heron
_____ jaguar	_____ coral snake	_____ bat
_____ monkey	_____ butterfly	_____ hummingbird
_____ wild pig	_____ panther	_____ ocelot

Booktalk

Welcome to the Greenhouse by Jane Yolen. Illustrated by Laura Regan. Putnam's, 1993.

   Here is the mysterious world of the tropical rain forest, a house where giant forest trees form the walls, and vines frame the views, and there is no roof overhead, only a canopy of leaves. Everywhere color threads through the hot greenhouse. By day you can hear exotic noises, the rustling of the green-coated sloth, or the chatter of monkeys as they make their way from room to room. A flash of the hummingbird or the silver streak of a lizard catch the eye and the ear picks up the crunch of the wild pig as it bites into tropical fruit. Listen carefully for the wings of the heron flapping to take off in flight, the swoop of the bat as it glides by the sleeping ocelot and hear the prowling panther searching for its dinner.

   Welcome to the greenhouse.
   Welcome to the hot house.
   Welcome to the land of the warm, wet days.

A Writing Activity

Pretend you have stepped into the rain forest. Complete the following lines about your experience.

Into the tropical rain forest

Over _____

Under _____

Above _____

Between _____

Lives a _____

The Arctic

Pre-Reading Activity: Before hearing the booktalk, work with a partner to answer these questions yes or no. *Guess* if you do not know.

_____ 1. Three arctic mammals are the fox, hare and seal.
_____ 2. Poppies grow in the Arctic.
_____ 3. Polar bears cannot swim.

Booktalk

Arctic Spring by Sue Vyner. Illustrated by Tim Vyner. Viking, 1993.

Spring has finally come to the Arctic, bringing warmth and sunlight and a special surprise. The long Arctic winter is over at last. The hare hops out of his hole, the fox emerges from his lair, and the seal surfaces from under the ice. Even the poppies are growing in the snow.

But the polar bear remains close by her den, even when the ice it is built on begins to drift away from land. She could swim to safety before the warm sun melts the ice, but she does not move. She stays close to her den. What could she be guarding so faithfully? To find out, read *Arctic Spring*.

A Writing Activity

Find information about one of the Arctic animals and use this pattern to write about it.

One spring morning you look out your window and see (describe an Arctic scene)_____. And there, coming from behind a snow drift is a/an (animal) _____. Its coat is _____ and it moves (how) _____ like a _____. The (animal) _____ is hungry and searches for _____. There is movement everywhere. Spring has come to the Arctic!

The Arctic

Before hearing the booktalk, answer the following statements yes or no. Guess if you do not know.

_____	1.	Caribou circle to protect themselves.
_____	2.	Wolves live in packs.
_____	3.	A healthy caribou can outrun a wolf.
_____	4.	Wolves eat caribou.
_____	5.	A two-year-old wolf cannot survive alone.
_____	6.	Wolves live in the Arctic.

Booktalk

The Call of the Wolves by Jim Murphy. Scholastic, 1992.

The raw Arctic wind blew down from the mountains. The old wolf was troubled. Snow was coming and the caribou were on the move. The pack, males, females and pups had to follow. The wolves spread out to attack the circled caribou herd. They were seeking a weak caribou, for a healthy one can outrun a wolf. The pack moved in for the kill. Suddenly a plane dipped toward the herd. Shots rang out. One of the young wolves broke away and ran until he dropped with exhaustion. While he slept, the snow came, and when he awoke the wolf pack was gone. The young wolf was alone and did not have the knowledge or experience to survive. His howls echoed from the mountain peaks. Would he survive or would this be his last winter? The two-year-old stood and shook the snow from his back.

Data Bank -Wolves

Eats	Lives	Has	Does
moose	in packs	fear of man	hunts to eat
caribou	wilderness	thick fur	kills old animals
deer	Arctic	pointed ears	shares work
rabbits	National Parks	long tail	talks with ears
			roams, growls

Use the data bank to complete this pattern.

You are changing, changing

You feel _____

You are (two adjectives) _____

You (two verb phrases) _____

You are (size and shape) _____

and you are (participle & prepositional phrase) _____

You do not walk upright anymore as you (three verbs) _____

_____

It is (adjective) _____ to move like this, so (one

adjective and one simile) _____. You are

(name the animal) _____.

25

A Fact You Should Know

Twenty two billion tons of pollution are dumped into oceans every year.

From: *Protecting Rivers and Seas* by Kamini Khanduri. Usborne, 1991.

The Ocean

Pre-Reading Activity: Work with a friend or small group and guess where in the world each of these creatures might be found.

1. sea otter
2. green sea turtle
3. penguins
4. fur seal
5. polar bear
6. humpback whale

a. _____ all the world's oceans

b. _____ Oregon coast

c. _____ Antarctica

d. _____ Costa Rica

e. _____ Canada

f. _____ Chile

Booktalk

World Water Watch by Michelle Koch. Greenwillow, 1993.

"Watch over the world, watch over the water, some creatures are dying today." Sea otters off the Oregon, Washington and California coasts, green sea turtles on the beaches of Florida, Mexico and Costa Rica; the penguins of Antarctica; the fur seal of the coast of Chile; polar bears of Denmark, Canada, Norway and Russia; and humpback whales in all the world's oceans are some of the many creatures of the world that are in danger. In this picture book for the youngest environmentalist you will learn where these creatures live, their habits and needs, and about the human hazards that threaten them.

The Ocean

A Research Project: The Mystery Report

Choose one of the endangered animals from *World Water Watch* and find ten facts about it. List the ten facts in random order. One fact must be a "give away" fact..one that will easily identify the animal.

EXAMPLE:

1. Sometimes my home moves.
2. At times I am seen as far south as the Gulf of St. Lawrence.
3. I can grow to be nine and one half feet long.
4. When fully grown I weigh about 1000 pounds.
5. I give birth to only one or two young at a time.
6. Seals are my favorite food.
7. In the winter I live in an ice cave.
8. I am a powerful swimmer.
9. My coat is white fur tinged with yellow.
10. I am found in Canada, Norway, Russia, Alaska, Greenland and Siberia.

Play the Mystery Game

One student in the group says a number between one and ten. The clue for that number is read. The student can guess the animal or pass. If the student passes or does not guess correctly, then another student can give a number. The game continues until the animal is guessed or all numbers are used.

Answer: Polar Bear.

Plant Life

Work with a partner to mark these statements yes or no. Then read the booktalk to support or deny your guesses.

_____ 1. When you pinch Touch-Me-Not seed pods, the seeds pop out.

_____ 2. Indians used Mullen leaves to keep their feet warm.

_____ 3. People in Ireland think dandelion juice cures warts.

Booktalk

A Child's Book of Wildflowers by M.A. Kelly. Illustrated by Joyce Powzyk. Four Winds Press, 1993. (Grades 2-6)

It is as near as your backyard, as close as the empty lot at the end of the block or the meadow out behind the barn. It is as easy as blowing dandelion puffs on a summer day, as lively as the seeds that pop out of Touch-Me-Nots, as fascinating as the face of a sunflower. Welcome to the world of wildflowers where the Irish find a cure for warts in dandelion juice and Indians survived the cold with Mullen leaves. From Bouncing Bet to goldenrod to evening primrose, here is a guide to the myth and history surrounding these plants.

Activity

Take a guess...How were these plants used long ago......???

Match the plant with a use people have found for it.

Plant		Use
_____ milkweed	1.	soap
_____ pokeweed	2.	glue
_____ mint	3.	bath
_____ Bouncing Bet	4.	salad
_____ chicory	5.	paint

These and many other uses for wildflowers can be found in this book.

Answers: milkweed (2), pokeweed (5), mint (3), Bouncing Bet (1), chicory (4)

A Fact You Should Know

In 1991 in the United States, 462 plant and animal species were endangered.

From: *Endangered Species* by C. Lampton Wallis, 1988.

Rivers

Pre-Reading Activity: Before hearing the booktalk, put a *J* in front of any word below that would be found in a jungle; a *D* in front of things found in the desert; an *I* in front of things found in a tropical island and an *M* in front of things found on a mountain.

_____ 1. lupine   _____ 2. lions   _____ 3. coconut

_____ 4. cockatoos   _____ 5. jasmine   _____ 6. mother-of-pearl

_____ 7. kangaroos   _____ 8. camels   _____ 9. monkey

Booktalk

Miss Rumphius by Barbara Cooney. Viking, 1982. (Grades K-3)

Miss Rumphius's first name was Alice and when she was small she dreamed of travelling to faraway places and living by the sea. Her grandfather told her that she must also make the world a more beautiful place in which to live.

Miss Rumphius *did* travel to far away places and saw coconuts and cockatoos on tropical islands, lions in the grasslands and monkeys in the jungle. On a hillside she found lupine and jasmines growing and rode a camel across the desert to meet a kangaroo in an Australian town.

Yes, Miss Rumphius did almost everything she wanted to do. In her later years she even lived by the sea. But what could she do to make the world a more beautiful place? To find out read, *Miss Rumphius*.

What ideas do you have for Miss Rumphius to make the world more beautiful?

A Writing Activity

In this book you will discover that Alice's favorite flower is the lupine. Here is an acrostic poem that describes the lupine. Choose your favorite flower and write an acrostic poem about it.

     L upines are beautiful flowers that bloom
     U p after you
     P lant the seed
     I n the ground. One day you
     N otice their beautiful rose and purple colors, but
     E ventually they will begin to wilt.

A Fact You Should Know

Rabbits brought to Australia from England bred so fast that they ate crops and harmed habitats of many other animals.

From: *Protecting Endangered Species* by Felicity Brooks. Usborne, 1990.

Ecosystems

Pre-Reading Activity: What do we know about ecosystems? Before hearing the booktalk, work with a partner to answer these questions yes or no.

1. _____ Milk is a nutritious food.
2. _____ Cows eat sweet red clover.
3. _____ Bees carry pollen.
4. _____ Mice eat honeycombs.
5. _____ Cats chase mice.

Booktalk

The Old Ladies Who Liked Cats by Carol Greene. Illustrated by Loretta Krupinski. HarperCollins, 1991.

On a small island lived some ladies who liked cats for the cats made the island a safe place to live. These ladies let their cats out at night to chase mice who would otherwise eat the bees' honeycombs. The bees carry pollen that makes the clover grow. The clover feeds the cows who give milk to keep the sailors who protect the island strong and healthy.

However, when the Mayor makes a new law not allowing cats out at night the whole balance of nature is disturbed and invaders come and take over the island. When the Mayor finally realizes how important the cats are he changes the law and life gets back to normal.

A Writing Activity

Could you write a story using this set of facts?

New Zealand flatworms were brought to Ireland in potted plants. They escaped into the wild and multiplied so fast that they killed the earthworms needed to keep the soil healthy. With poor soil Irish potatoes, a main crop and food for many people, will not grow.

Ecosystems
The Old Ladies Who Liked Cats (continued)

Writing About Elements in an Ecosystem

Choose an ecosystem element from the story to write about:

cats   clover   bees
mice   cows   honeycombs

Find out:

Color _____

Where found _____

Covered with _____

Eats (or eaten by) _____

How it moves (animal) _____

Enemies _____

Use your information in a pattern like the one below:

I saw a MOUSE and the MOUSE saw me. It was SKITTERING by an island tree. MOUSE goes HONEY, HONEY FOR ME.

I saw _____ and _____ saw me. It

was _____ by the island's trees

_____ goes

_____ for me.

People and Wildlife

Heron Street by Ann Turner. HarperCollins, 1989.

Before hearing the booktalk, discuss this question with a small group.

What happens to wild animals when people come and build houses and roads in the places where the animals lived? Give at least four answers.

Booktalk

"In the beginning they lived in a marsh by the sea—herons, ducks, geese raccoons. Rattlesnakes and wolves lived along its drier edge.

Sqwonk-honk, chee-hsis, aroooo! And the wind in the tall grass sang, "Shhh-hello, hsss-hello."

But then men and woman and children came and everything began to change. They built houses and churches and made roads through the marsh. Slowly, as time passed and there was more building up and tearing down, the animals began to leave in search of wilder lands to live in. Here is a tale of progress, the losses it has caused in nature, and the wonders it has made possible for people.

A Writing Activity

Follow this pattern to write about the effect of progress on wildlife. Try to end your story on a positive note.

FORTUNATELY: The first settlers built houses in the wilderness to shelter their families from the cold winter.

UNFORTUNATELY: The houses were built in a place wolves used as their home.

FORTUNATELY: The wolves found another wilderness area to live in until....

UNFORTUNATELY: More people came and built roads and cleared the forests for farms.

People and Wildlife

Screen of Frogs by Sheila Hamanaka. Orchard, 1993.

Readers Theatre Booktalk

Narrator One:	For the years of his youth Koji thought only of himself.
Koji:	Never of the mountains, lakes and fields
Narrator One:	that he had inherited.
Koji:	Never of the bees and birds, the woodcutters and peasants
Narrator One:	for whom his lands are home. He sold all he owned
Koji:	except for one mountain
Narrator One:	and was about to sell that when he
Frogs:	was visited by
Narrator Two:	the frogs who told him
Frogs:	what would happen if all the trees were cut down.
Narrator Two:	The frogs are grateful that Koji listened to them.
Frogs:	Can you tell why???

Recipe for Destroying the Earth

Take one mountain

Cut down all the trees

Chase away the birds, the bees

and the fox

Add the sun to dry the soil

Add rain to wash the earth into streams

and lakes

Flood the land...Destroy all life.

A Fact You Should Know

Young black bears are being forced out of their home territories by older males and have no place to go, thus end up wandering into nearby towns.
From: *Backyard Bear* by Jim Murphy. Scholastic, 1993.

People and Wildlife

Predict what might happen if a bear entered your yard late one night.

1. _____
2. _____
3. _____

Booktalk

Backyard Bear by Jim Murphy. Illustrated by Jeffrey Greene. Scholastic, 1993.

It's a dark, moonlit night when the hungry young bear pauses at the foot of the mountain. To cross the ribbon of asphalt separating his forest from the town below is to trespass. But the delicious smell of food is too inviting and, a second later, he crosses the road and enters the sleeping town.

He wanders from one back yard to another going deeper and deeper into a strange and scary world. And when a sudden noise startles the townspeople awake, what had been a harmless search for food becomes a frightening chase. Will the young bear escape the humans who are determined to catch him? To find out read, *Backyard Bear*.

A Research Model

Collect interesting facts about many kinds of bears and compile a Fact or Fiction Book About Bears. On one page make a statement about bears. On the next page tell your reader whether the statement is fact or fiction and why.

Fact or Fiction?	Fiction
Siberian brown bears eat fish whole.	Siberian brown bears eat only fish heads and throw the rest away.

People and Wildlife

In *Backyard Bear* the brown bear was driven away from the forest by older, larger bears.

In China the Giant Panda was driven out of its bamboo forests which were cleared to make room for farms.

Animals disappearing from the earth are called endangered.

Guess: Which of these animals is endangered right now?

_____ lemurs	_____ Mountain Gorillas	_____ tiger
_____ cheetah	_____ Peregrine falcon	_____ leopard
_____ rhino	_____ grizzly bear	_____ elephant

The correct answer is ALL of these animals are endangered.

Choose an endangered animal to write about. Find out where it lives, what it looks like and how it moves. Use the information in the pattern poem below.

EXAMPLE:

Animal name: Elephant
How it moves: Lumbering   Plodding
Where: In Asian teak forests
Where: In the African grasslands
Describe: Gray Giant!

Animal name: _____

How it moves: _____   _____

Where: _____

Where: _____

Describe: _____

> ## A Fact You Should Know
> Scientists believe that by the year 2000, 25,000 different kinds of plants which now exist will be no longer found on the earth.
> From: *Protecting Endangered Species* by Felicity Brooks. Usborne, 1990.

People and Nature

Before hearing the booktalk, complete this poem with signs of spring.

On the first day of spring,
What did I see but a _____
Looking at me.

On the second day of spring,
What did I see but a _____
Nodding at me.

On the third day of spring,
What did I see but a _____
Waving at me.

On the fourth day of spring,
What did I see but a _____
Winking at me.

On the fifth day of spring,
What did I see but a _____
_____ at me.

After hearing the booktalk about *The Lorax*, look again at your completed poem. How would the signs of spring change if all the trees were cut down?

EXAMPLE:

On the first day of spring,
What did I see but a barren land
Looking at me.

People and Nature

Booktalk

The Lorax by Dr. Seuss. Random House, 1971.

A visitor arrives in a barren land and finds only an old "Once-ler" living there. It seems that many years before, the land was filled with beautiful Truffula trees, clear ponds, clean clouds and happy animals. Then one by one the trees were cut down to make products for people. A Lorax visited the Once-lers who were destroying the trees and warned them that all of the animals would disappear. The Once-lers ignored the warning until the last tree was cut down. The air was filled with factory smoke. The ponds were full of glump. The birds and animals were gone. With a sad face the Lorax takes leave of the polluted land leaving a small pile of rocks with just one word: UNLESS!

Discussion

Work with a group of three or four students. Each group should have a secretary or recorder to write the main ideas of the group. In ten minutes list as many ways as you can that the barren "Grickle grass" part of town in this story could be made green and clean once again. Share your list with others in the class. Complete this sentence with your best idea.

The barren land that the Lorax left will stay that way unless

_____

_____

A Fact You Should Know
Americans throw away about 40 billion soft drink cans and bottles each year.
From: *Going Green* by John Elkington. Viking, 1990.

Pollution

Pre-Reading Activity: Before hearing the booktalk, mark each word
below with the letter *P* if the words gives you a positive feeling and with
the letter *N* if the word gives you a negative feeling.

1. ____ potbellied   4. ____ gobbling   6. ____ grassy
2. ____ machines   5. ____ grinding   7. ____ cavern
3. ____ leafy   8. ____ meadow

Booktalk

The Wump World written and illustrated by Bill Peet. Houghton Mifflin,
1970.

The Wumps live in a world of grassy meadows and leafy green trees
surrounded by winding rivers and lakes. It is a happy, pleasant world
until one day a great flock of potbellied monsters land in the meadow
and belch forth pollutions with their giant machines. The Wumps
tumble down into a dark cavern as the machines gobble trees and
grind them to bits. The Pollutions were constructing their "wonderful
new world." Meanwhile, the Wumps remained underground frightened
by the endless noises. Would the Wumps ever see their beautiful world
again?

A Thinking and Writing Activity

The Three Rs of keeping the Earth clean are:
REUSE   RECYCLE   REFUSE
Describe one way you can use each of the three Rs to help keep the
Earth clean.

I could REUSE _____
by _____
instead of throwing it away.

I could RECYCLE _____
by _____
instead of _____

I could REFUSE to _____
and the result would be _____
_____

Another Bill Peet book with a similar story is *Farewell to Shady Glade*
(Houghton-Mifflin, 1966). Compare these two books for characters,
setting, problem and solution.   38

Pollution

Booktalk

The World That Jack Built written and illustrated by Ruth Brown. E.P. Dutton, 1991.

This tale begins with a beautiful world of green grass, budding blossoms, growing forests, clear streams and buttercup meadows...all a part of the world that Jack built. Then with these words, the landscape changes: "These are the hills that form the valley next to the one...that Jack built." The hills are black, the forest burnt away, the meadows are bare and mud packed, the streams are polluted and flow "past the place where the trees used to grow, next to the factory that Jack built."

Find books in your library that tell what you can do to help keep the world clean and green. Choose three things you plan to do and tell about them in the poem that follows:

If I were in charge of keeping the world clean

I would _____

and _____

because _____

_____

But the most important thing I would do to keep the world clean would be _____

_____

If I were in charge of keeping the world clean.

A Fact You Should Know

In one year the typical American family throws out 2,460 pounds of paper, 480 pounds of glass and 480 pounds of food scraps.

From *Going Green* by John Elkington. Viking, 1990.

Solutions

Pre-Reading Activity: Before hearing the booktalk about how the citizens of Beaston solved their trash problem, answer yes or no to the following questions.

1. _____ Incinerators are good because they burn trash and make energy.
2. _____ A good way to get rid of trash is to dump it in the ocean.
3. _____ Food scraps turn into soil in a compost bin.
4. _____ One way to solve the trash problem is to buy products in returnable containers.

Booktalk

A Great Trash Bash by Loreen Leedy. Holiday House, 1991.

The Mayor of Beaston can't figure out what is wrong with the town until one day he slips on a banana peel and realizes the town has too much trash. A town meeting is called and all the citizens put their heads together to solve the problem. They decide that incinerators burn trash and create energy but cause air pollution. Trash dumped in the ocean pollutes the water. The only answer is to change the way they live. They learn to buy products in returnable containers, to return food scraps to soil in compost bins, and to reuse rather than to buy new things. The citizens of Beaston learn to be real trash bashers!

Solutions
The Great Trash Bash (continued)

Write a Limerick

A limerick is a nonsense verse that has five lines. The first and second lines rhyme, the third and fourth lines rhyme and the fifth line usually ends in a surprise statement that rhymes with the first line.

The citizens of Beaston found many things they could do to solve their trash problems. Some of these were:

reuse	buy in bulk	stop littering
compost	fix the old	recycle

Use one of these solutions in a limerick to show how you can bash trash in your community.

EXAMPLE:

One way to bash trash is reuse
You surely have nothing to lose,
You'll find the good news
For you who reuse
Is money to use as you choose.

_____

_____

_____

_____

_____

Solutions

Booktalk

Going Green: A Kid's Handbook to Saving the Planet by John Elkington, Julia Hailes, Douglas Hill , and Joel Makower. Illustrated by Tony Ross. Viking, 1990.

With so many big problems facing our planet, you might not think that you can make a difference. But everything you do has an effect on the environment, even things as simple as buying a can of soda or brushing your teeth. You CAN help save the environment, and *Going Green* shows you how.

Simple explanations of such problems as the greenhouse effect, our vanishing rain forests, and energy use and misuse bring the most pressing environmental issues into focus.

You'll learn about the three Rs: REUSE and RECYCLE as much as you can, and REFUSE to buy environmentally unsafe products; how to conduct a green audit of your home, school and community; and projects you can do to solve the problems you discover. Amazing facts keep you on the green track to help ensure a safer, healthier planet for today and tomorrow. Now's the time to join the Green Team!

A Thinking and Writing Project

Compose a class book "Saving the Planet from A-Z".

For each letter of the alphabet list something you can do to make our planet safer and healthier.

See the ABC section of *Going Green* for ideas!

Index To Titles